I WI...
N...

SEEK ME

CRYSTAL CATTABRIGA

Seek Me © 2024 by Crystal Cattabriga

All rights reserved and printed in the United States of America.

No part of this book may be used or reproduced in any manner whatsoever without written permission except in the case of brief quotations embodied in critical articles and reviews.

Crystal Cattabriga Publishing, Georgia

E-book: 979-8-9900588-2-8

Paperback: 979-8-9900588-1-1

Hardcover: 979-8-9900588-0-4

Unless otherwise indicated, all Scriptures quotations are taken from The Holy Bible, HOLMAN CHRISTIAN STANDARD BIBLE copyright© 1999, 2000, 2002, 2003 by Holman Bible Publishers, Nashville, Tennessee. All rights reserved.

Cover Design: Under Cover Designs

Library of Congress Cataloging-in-Publication data is available.

Dedication

My Lord and Savior Jesus Christ.

Psalm 46:5

"God is within her; she will not fail."

In Memory of Zack Cothran

Psalm 118:8

"It is better to take refuge in the Lord than to trust in humanity."

Pastor Josh Taylor

Matthew 10:7

As you go, proclaim, 'The kingdom of heaven has come near.'

My family and friends

Numbers 6:24-26

"May the Lord bless you and protect you; may the Lord make his face shine on you; and be gracious to you; may the Lord look with favor on you and give you peace.

Foreword by Gail Durbin

Proverbs 31:26-31

"Her mouth speaks wisdom, and loving instruction is on her tongue. She watches over the activities of her household and is never idle. Her children rise up and call her blessed; her husband also praises her: "Many women have done noble deeds, but you surpass them all!" Charm is deceptive and beauty is fleeting, but a woman who fears the Lord will be praised. Give her the reward of her labor, and let her works praise her at the city gates."

This scripture embodies the author and my friend Crystal. She is intelligent, loving, and blessed. Her husband praises her, and she fears the Lord. Our friendship is centered and grounded in Jesus Christ. From the moment we met, her love for the Lord was evident, and I wanted that same love and joy that she exuded. If you could actually "hear" her telling this story, you would see her contagious love for Christ that so many people (Christians) today are lacking.

This book reminds us that we should seek Him daily in all our lives. From beginning to end, she will captivate you with her journey to the Savior!

Introduction

Seek Me is a spiritual book on how to grow in love with Jesus Christ.

A compass that guides and reminds us that we are sons and daughters of the highest. Just as it has been proclaimed in **1Peter 2:9,** "But you are a chosen race, a royal priesthood, a holy nation, a people for his possession, so that you may claim the praises of the one who called you out of darkness into his marvelous light." This world is temporary until we reunite with the Father in heaven, and oh, what a glorious day that will be.

In the meantime, we need to make much of Jesus. Taking risks that may be uncomfortable for our Savior is the least we can do. Excitement, tensions, and conflicts might arise on the battlefield for Christ, but we are taught to take up our cross. We must remember that Christ is not just Sunday and Wednesday. He is every day.

When I decided to write this book, I contemplated giving my entire testimony, being vulnerable and raw to the core. I realized the best way for you to understand why I love

Christ is to do just that: tell the story of me. This experience has allowed me to love God more deeply. It's drawn me closer to Him, and I want that for you.

My heart and mind have been flooded with love since I gave my life to Christ. I still have good and bad days, just like anyone else, but life is more manageable when I can lay my burdens at the foot of the cross, knowing Jesus will make a way. I pray that this book brings you closer to Him. I pray that you come to know Him in a way that will allow peace, joy, and happiness.

1. Testimony

Psalm 66:16

"Come and listen, all who fear God, and I will tell what he has done for me."

Child of God

John 1:12-13, "But to all who did receive him, he gave them the right to be children of God, to those who believe in his name, who were born, not of natural descent, or of the will of the flesh, or of the will of man, but of God."

On April 1, 1976, I took my first breath.

Job 33:4, "The Spirit of God has made me, and breath of the Almighty gives me life."

Psalm 139:13, *"For it was you who created my inward parts; you knit me together in my mother's womb."*

Had I read this scripture years ago and not known Jesus as I do now, I would have held Him responsible for what would come in 1978. I have no recollection of the events leading up to and during the moment my family's life and faith were tested when the pediatrician said, "Your daughter needs Open Heart Surgery." What I do know is that I have a permanent scar that will be with me always.

As a parent of three, I can't imagine hearing those words about one of my children. The emotions that consumed my parents were overwhelming. It wasn't until I was brought to Boston Children's Hospital that Dr. Aldo Castaneda from Cardiology would hit my parents with a 1-2 punch, giving them more excruciating news about their daughter. "With any surgery, there are risks such as bleeding, blood clots, failure of the replacement valve, infection, stroke, death, but if we don't perform the surgery, she may not live a long life," he informed them.

Dr. Castaneda explained that I had what's called Pulmonary valve regurgitation. Simply put, it is a leaky pulmonary valve that allows blood to flow backward into the heart rather than directly to the lungs for oxygen. However, there was no guarantee of what would happen, so my parents decided to go forward with the surgery. I was told it took three hours to perform. Using a scalpel, the surgeon (Dr. Castaneda) cut through my sternum eight to ten inches. Prying my chest open, I was then connected to a heart-lung bypass machine.

This machine moves blood away from the heart so the surgeon can operate. Taking a vein from my inner thigh it was then placed in my chest to repair my leak. Once the medical team could tell everything went well, my sternum was wired together before sewing my skin back. My hospital stay was just over forty days.

A year had gone by, and I was due back at the hospital to make sure my new valve was working correctly. The news wasn't exactly what my parents hoped for. The valve the doctor repaired was functioning as it should, but now my Mitral valve was leaking. The human heart has four valves. Each time the heart beats, these valves open and close to let blood in and out of the chambers. My right chamber had been fixed, but the left chamber was leaking. Talk about bad luck.

Dr. Castaneda informed my parents that performing another surgery would be too risky. He assured my parents that I should grow up healthy but would have restrictions such as don't run a marathon and no children. These things could put further strain on my valve, tearing it more. Did it stop me from running a marathon? Yes, but walking several

5k's? Nope! Did it stop me from having three beautiful children? Not at all.

Psalm 34:17-18

"The righteous cry out, and the Lord hears, and rescues them from all their troubles."

<u>Abuse</u>

Child abuse comes in several different forms, including physical, emotional, sexual, and psychological abuse. The memories of my childhood seem to fade as I become older. I want to claim that it's because of my age, but I often associate it more with the fact that some of the trauma I experience prevents any joyful memories from surfacing. From a young teenager up until my late twenties, I was discarded and unwanted, so it was hard for me to fully trust when I became an adult and the relationships I encountered.

I am not here to point fingers at those who wronged me. I am forgiving you. It took years for me to know my worth. The simple truth is that sometimes the abuser abuses because they were abused themselves. This doesn't excuse their actions; it just sheds light on what caused all the abuse in the first place.

There are many articles written by individuals with degrees stating that abuse and divorce will be detrimental to a child growing up. I credit those who have spent years studying human behavior, but I believe the average person without a degree has reached the same conclusion. The question is, how can we break the cycle? I will never claim to have all the answers to many problems, but I know where we can start. I'll get to that later on.

Psalm 27:10 *"Even if my mother and father abandon me, the Lord cares for me."*

Foster Care

At the age of sixteen, I needed a way out. My life felt worthless. I had little left inside me and didn't care if I walked this earth another day. Many times, I wanted the ground to open up and swallow me. I was suffering in silence. I was the warden, guard, and prisoner of my thoughts. There were many nights I would lay on my bed staring up at the ceiling, thinking, "How is it fair that the sins of another lay upon me.?" It is never okay for a child to bear the weight of another person's horrific acts, never mind into adulthood.

My innocence as a child was stolen at a young age, so the only place left for me was away from it all. I knew running was the only way to find my place. The only two choices were to be homeless or in the system (foster care). I chose the latter because going back home was no longer an option. In the end, both would become part of my story.

The woman who became my guardian in foster care briefly had a soft-spoken voice with kind eyes. This was the first time I felt safe until I was asked to leave. I don't recall how long I was placed there, but I know it was not long. Seeing this was over thirty years ago, I cannot remember the woman's name, so we will call her Mrs. Moore. I recall her telling me she had been married for many years, and if I saw an older gentleman sneak in late, that was him.

I saw him heading to the den several times toward the back of the house, where he would fall asleep in his recliner. Mrs. Moore had two grandchildren who also lived there. Her granddaughter and I were the same age and attended the same school, yet we didn't know each other nor hang in the same circle of friends. I ended up sharing a bedroom downstairs with her, while Mrs. Moore's grandson, who was in college, had a bedroom in the attic. Things were good for a while until they weren't.

Mrs. Moore's granddaughter and I did not get along, which made things difficult, and on top of that, I had lost one of the most amazing people who meant the world to me while I was there. I'll never forget the day the phone rang, and a family member somehow found out where I was placed.

"Crystal, this is." I quickly interject and say, "I know who this is; why are you calling me?"

"I am sorry to tell you that your Uncle Mike has died."

The only thing I recall after that was that I found myself walking down one of the side streets next to the house, wondering what happened. I found out sometime later that my uncle died of Aids. There was no funeral—just a simple cremation. My heart ached for years, never being able to see him one last time. Soon after that, things started to go downhill quickly, and I was asked to leave my foster home.

To make a long story short, Mrs. Moore's granddaughter and I got into a fistfight, which understandably was not tolerated. I'm sure Mrs. Moore knew her granddaughter instigated the fight, but I politely excused myself from her home. Deep down inside, I knew she was heartbroken that things had to be this way, but I assured her that in the short time I was there, she did her best and made me feel like part of her family.

Where would I go to next?

The Streets

Being homeless or crashing on someone's couch seemed more accepting than home. The thought of feeling rejected over and over consumed me like a flesh-eating plague, and I couldn't handle it. I needed a purpose. I needed a reason to exist. When the darkness inhabited my thoughts, becoming too much to bear, I would stroll between cities, randomly finding cemeteries and reading headstones as though I was looking for a particular person, but I wasn't. Whenever I encountered a person's life that didn't make it past twenty-five, I would sit in front of it, wondering how their life was cut short. Other times, I would think, why couldn't it be me instead? Then I wouldn't feel sad anymore.

Days turned into weeks, and weeks became months, wondering where I would end up when the sun went down and whether I would be safe. I'll be honest: Some places I stayed in would make the average person return home. Night after night, I struggled to understand how a middle-class kid from a small town could be rejected and unwanted. Again, I am not blaming a specific person; the house I grew up just wasn't home.

Looking back on the life I lived as a young teenager into my early twenties, I can say without a doubt that I should've died several times over. It has taken years for me to be able to look in a mirror to see my worth. No one should have to experience most of the things I endured growing up. When people go through trauma, they try to lock it away, and that's what I did for so long. Denying it is easier than facing it head-on.

After several months of couch surfing, I found a safe place to lay my head. A family member, whom I'll keep anonymous, discovered that I'd been discarded like yesterday's trash and took me in. This person, I honestly believe, was heartbroken that I had been living, or shall I say, surviving this way. I didn't stay exceedingly long, not because I didn't get three meals a day, a warm place to sleep, or told I was loved because I did. I left because my burdens weren't theirs to bear. It took me years to realize that only one person could bear my burdens, and His name is Jesus.

First Marriage

This was short-lived. Looking back at my first marriage, I believe we were both to blame. He was an unfaithful husband, and yet I came to realize it was more my fault than his. I know what you're thinking. I'm crazy, so let me explain. Going back some years, I had been in an eight-and-a-half-year relationship with a man. We had a child together six years into the relationship. I wanted to be married, but he didn't. I left. Fast forward a few years later.

In the summer of 1997, I attended my cousin's wedding. That's where I would reconnect with a childhood friend. I'm not entirely sure how it all happened, but three months later, we married—now going back to where I take more of the blame for why my marriage ended after only nine months. This is me bearing my soul. He asked. I said yes, but I never really loved him the way someone should when they marry.

Did it hurt when I found out that he was unfaithful to me with another woman? Of course. Did I want to inflict pain on him? Sure. Did I? No. With everything I had gone through growing up, you would think this would have done me in, but it didn't. Instead, it brought me to a place where loving someone and trusting again became even more complicated.

Jeremiah 17:14 *"Heal me, Lord, and I will be healed; save me, and I will be saved, for you are my praise."*

Appendix, Abortion, and Cancer

My health and mental state had been tested. Everything that could be thrown at me was when I had three medical scares within a year and a half. My appendix ruptured back in. "2000." I had been having excruciating pain for a few days, but I didn't want to go to the hospital. I figured whatever it was, it would pass, but by the fourth day, I ended up in the ER in the middle of the night.

The first hospital I went to that was close to my house had a wait time of two hours. I remember looking at the receptionist saying, "No disrespect, but I don't think I have two hours." She apologized and said there was nothing she could do for me. I would have to take a seat and wait my turn. My body was telling me I didn't have two hours, so instead, my friend drove me thirty minutes to another hospital.

When I arrived, I explained what was going on to the receptionist. She politely told me it might be a bit before they could get me in a room. My options were limited, so I stayed. After filling out the forms and handing them back to me, she looked at me and asked, "Are you related to Donna?" I replied, "Yes." Quickly, she waved down a nurse, telling her to grab a wheelchair and bring me to the room across the hall.

Let me stop here and explain. It had been over a year since my divorce, and I had met someone else who, down the road, would be my now husband of twenty-one years. Most of his family were medical professionals, a state trooper, and a fire department captain, which helped. It was a miracle for me that his aunt had been a nurse for over thirty years at Toby Hospital, where I ended up that night. I'm not going to lie; I felt like royalty then. The saying is true. It helps to know people. That night, knowing Donna saved my life.

Come to find out; my appendix had burst several days before, causing an infection throughout my abdomen, resulting in a condition medically called Peritonitis. It is life-threatening and requires me to have emergency surgery. As

I was being brought into the operating room, I started throwing up uncontrollably and spiking a fever. This resulted because morphine was administered to me. Had the male nurse read my paperwork, he would have known that I could not have morphine because I was allergic to it. By God's grace and quick-acting nurses and doctors, they saved me, and so did Donna. I chose not to take legal action. I was just grateful that I pulled through that night.

In February 2002, I married again, but this time to the man whose aunt helped save my life. This was not my intention, yet I couldn't shake the feeling that this would be my forever love, so I said yes. My husband and I talked about having a child, and after several months of deep discussions, we became pregnant with our daughter. This journey became a test of our love for each other and my faith in what God would see me through.

During one of my routine visits early on at the OBGYN, I was told I might need to go to Brigham and Women in Rhode Island. I had already done at least a handful of pap smears, and none returned normal. My doctor explained that it was best for me to have some of my cells tested further to know exactly what we were dealing with. Off I went to

Rhode Island. Week after week, I endured several more pap smears. Somewhere between the tenth pap smear, I received a call back asking to come in to hear and discuss my options.

Over the years, I've heard people say they've experienced doctors with poor bedside manners; I now understand their disgust. I experienced it firsthand that day. Being just under four months pregnant and not knowing what to expect, I would have hoped for a better outcome or at least someone with compassion. That didn't happen. My husband and I sat in the waiting room until my name was called. What seemed like forever had only been ten minutes before I noticed the nurse opening the door and calling my name.

My husband asked if I wanted him to go with me, but I felt this was something I had to do on my own. The nurse took me down a long hall and pointed to the door on the left, saying, "The doctor will be in a few minutes." Sitting in the chair against the pale-looking wall, I thought, whatever it was, it would be fine.

True confession- I knew of God but didn't proclaim Him nor live for Him at this time in my life, so who was I to ask Him to give me a miracle? And if I am honest, I never asked for one. I just sat patiently, waiting for the door to swing open so I could get this over with, whatever it was. I watched the clock on the wall tick until I heard the knock on the door that broke my rhythm. I answered, "Yes."

A tall, lanky man with thick Coke bottle glasses entered the room. Pulling out the small round stool from under the counter, he sat down, introducing himself. I leave his name out of the equation. Right away, I could tell he was the type to say he would count to three before ripping the band aide off but would do it on the count of one: no empathy or compassion. I know it's been years, but I can tell you precisely what he said because you never forget the hurtful words someone inflicts on you, but because of God's grace, you forgive.

"Mrs. Cattabriga, do you have any other child, or is this your first?" He asked.

"I have two boys," I replied.

This is where his horrible bedside manner came into play, "After several test and pap smears, you have abnormal cells at twelve, three, six, and nine that, if not removed, will become cancerous. My advice is to have an abortion, seeing you have two other children. Once removed, if you and your husband want to have another child, I believe you will be okay with doing so," he stated.

Yes, before giving my life to Jesus, I won't sugarcoat it. I didn't hold back that day telling him where he could go and what I thought of him. I wanted to punch him in the throat. I was angry. I was heartbroken. I was scared. I was appalled by what he thought I should do. Before storming out in tears, I asked him a straightforward question, "Will I die before giving birth from this cancer?"

Raising his eyebrows as if he were confused by the question or thought I was being ignorant, he replied, "No, but you'll have to endure chemo after delivering because you waited too long. Why would you want to put yourself through that?"

I knew he wouldn't comprehend what I was about to say, but I said it anyway. "I'm not going to end a life to save my own. A parent protects their child, and that's what I'm going to do: protect her." After that day, I never went back. I needed to choose my path once. I needed to feel in control of my life.

I understand that sometimes our actions can be a bit naïve, but I knew deep down inside that somehow I would survive and become a better person for the choice I made that day. My daughter is twenty-two, healthy, beautiful, and is engaged today. I took a risk, and I would do it again for her.

My truth:

You would be shocked to hear that I recently went to an OBGYN for the first time since that day, twenty-three years ago. Telling you this doesn't mean I'm invincible. It doesn't mean to ignore what your doctor might recommend. It just means that God's grace has been upon my life more times than I deserve. What are my test results today? The cells are still prominent but have never turned to cancer. That is a true testament to a miracle.

Luke 21:36 *"But be alert at all times, praying that you may have strength to escape all these things that are going to take place and stand before the Son of Man."*

Escape

Where does our strength come from? Some people believe it is in their DNA, and others believe it comes from

how they were raised. Amy Morin, therapist and author, states that there are three parts to mental state.
1. Thoughts
2. Feelings
3. Actions

Back in 2010, I took my family and escaped. Leaving behind one person whom I wished I had never left. I will not go into full details about why I needed to leave, but I will convey that the events that took place had we stayed would have left my family more broken than they already were. Before making this enormous decision that changed our lives, my thoughts became not my own anymore.

Everything I knew was no longer the truth, yet somehow, deep down, I knew the truth. It was just easier to deny what was being brought to the surface. My feelings were plagued with numbness, sadness, anger, fear, and worst of all, I became a victim of it all. The sins of another laid so heavy on me that I couldn't see the good in myself because of this individual who robbed me of my self-worth.

I know without question that we all have a soul. How? When you go through something so traumatic that it makes you want to scream, cry, hyperventilate, break anything, or wish the pain would stop, that's your inner soul broken. Being tormented by someone else's evil doing can wreck a person to their core. I was that person for so long. My actions would lead me to another state, trying to heal from what I genuinely believed had become Hell on Earth.

My family and I went to Georgia looking for a fresh start. It was a challenge to adjust at first. Leaving the North and living in the South was a culture shock, but the people here are loving. I never expected what I endured to keep me a victim forever. What robbed me of a life where I grew up no longer defines me.

We started a new chapter when we saw the sign, **"Welcome to Georgia."**

Ephesians 5:25 *"Husbands, love your wives, just as Christ loved the church and gave himself for her."*

I've lived in Georgia for twenty years, married, and have three grown adult children with four granddaughters. The road I have been on here has had difficulties. I thought my future would seem more manageable when I finally escaped the horror of my past. My husband and son butted heads over the years to the point that I found myself wanting out of my marriage more than I wanted to stay in it. In 2017, my marriage was on the brink of unrepairable.

The man who has loved me and brought me back to who I am today (a better version of myself) betrayed me for many years. It crushed my soul. When I say only God could repair the brokenness of my marriage, it is true. The scars I wear are just that—scars. I fought them on my knees in August of 2017 when I asked Christ to forgive me and heal me. Did I feel like I was alone before knowing Jesus? Absolutely.

I have only begun to scratch the surface of the life God has in store for me. Every little glimpse brings me closer to Christ. I don't need to see everything all at once. He knows what I need. What He wants is me. All of me, not part-time me. Worshiping a God who was, is, and will always be victorious is the best feeling. I will never live my life without Him.

Am I a sinner? Absolutely. Will I sin again? Absolutely. But I know the nailed-scarred hands that stretched out on an old-rugged cross was for me. He wiped it all away and continued to write my story. With this journey I have been on, God has always been there, even when I wasn't. My marriage was repaired and is stronger than ever. I want to say this: God loves you so much, created you in His image, and wants you to have happiness and peace in your heart.

If you are still trying to figure out Jesus, it's okay. No one has all the answers, but I want to clarify this question for non-believers the best way I can.

"Why would a loving God allow so much suffering."

I don't know why God allowed evil and suffering for thousands of years, and many theologians don't have the answer. As a follower of Christ, I can say that in the Book of Genesis, God intended all things to be good, but humans rebelled. We were born into a sinful world, which was a disadvantage for us. God gave us free will. Looking at The Ten Commandments, we know we should apply them to our lives. God doesn't make us; we choose.

For us to love freely, we must have free will. If it's not free, it's not love. Some people think that because Christians or followers of Christ speak of God being all-powerful, He can do anything He wants, but that's not what the Bible states. It means God has power over His creation, but He's chosen to limit his power and give us free will.

When we pray to the Almighty God, we are not praying to a faraway being. We are praying to a Father who loved us so much, even when we were sinners. Even when the world cursed His name, He put you in His focus, wrapping Himself up in human skin so He could meet people like you right where you are. When we pray to God, we do not pray to a creator. We pray to Emmanuel, who is with us. We pray to the one who's closer than a brother. When we deserve death, he says, "I will take your place." The wages of sin is death, but the gift of God is eternal life. The gift has a name, and it is Jesus.

He saved me!

2. Who is God?

God is the one who created the world—the one who first spoke it into existence—the one who made everything out of nothing, including man and woman. Genesis is the first book in the Bible. It gives us an insight into God's vision for the world. In six days, God made the heavens and the earth, which was good, but God wasn't finished yet. From His very own breath and dust from the ground, a man (Adam) was formed. It wasn't until later that God created a woman (Eve) from Adam's rib.

Genesis 2:24, "This is why a man leaves his father and mother and bonds with his wife, and they become one flesh." Adam and Eve would become husband and wife, living among all God made beautiful and perfect until the fall. It is written that in **Genesis 3:1- 24,** the serpent (devil), which God had made, tempted Eve into disobeying Him, and because of her selfishness, she defied God while convincing her husband to do the same.

The truth is that God gave them everything, yet they disobeyed Him, and because of this, **Romans 5:12** says, "Therefore, just as sin entered the world through one man, and death through sin, in this way death spread to all people because all sinned." As we read in The Old Testament, many people went against God. Moses wrote in **Deuteronomy 32:35**, "Vengeance and retribution belong to me. In time their foot will slip, for their day of disaster is near, and their doom is coming quickly," says the Lord. This reveals that God was not pleased with His people sinning.

As time passed, the earth became so corrupt of sin that God called upon a man named Noah. **Genesis 6:13** states that God declared, "I have decided to put an end to every creature, for the earth is filled with wickedness because of them; therefore I am going to destroy them along with the earth." God spared Noah and his family because Noah was a righteous man. Can you imagine what was going through Noah's mind when he was told that the earth would be wiped out? I'm sure Noah was grateful that he had been faithful to the Lord.

After the Flood, you would have thought things would have been different, but once again, sin spread like an infectious disease, causing God to rein on all who continue to disobey Him. We read in **Genesis 19:1-19** about the cities of Sodom and Gomorrah, how the people's sins included pride, homosexuality, and overabundance of food and wealth, and they did not care for the poor or needy. **Isaiah 3:9** and **Ezekial 16:49** also declare that not only were the people of Sodom and Gomorrah guilty of all those sins against God, but they were arrogant to think that their sins against God were not evil. In the end, God destroyed the cities by raining sulfur. What a tragedy.

The psalmist wrote in **Psalm 2:12,** "Pay homage to the Son or he will be angry and you will perish in your rebellion, for his anger may ignite at any moment. All who take refuge in him (God) are happy." **Genesis 15:6,** Abram believed the Lord, and he (God) credited it to him as righteous." The Lord loved and found favor in those who served Him.

Sin is grievous to God, and many still neglect His forewarning, paying the price. For those of God's people, many were not exempt from his judgment. In the book of **Exodus**, there were ten plagues God sent on Egypt because Pharoh wouldn't let the Israelites leave the nation. These plagues were blood, frogs, gnats, flies, livestock, boils, hail, locusts, darkness, and the firstborn.

The Lord's message to His people has always been evident. God has never made it difficult for you to seek Him.

For generations past, humanity has consistently pointed blame on why life is a struggle. In the New Testament, **Hebrews 10:1-18** states that sacrifices made under God's law could not save you. **Galatians 3:11** reveals, "Now it is clear that no one is justified before God by the law, because *the righteous will live by faith."*

Some might disagree with this and claim this scripture only applies to the New Testament, but Paul writes in **Habakkuk 2:4,** "Look, his ego is inflated; he is without integrity. But the righteous one will live by his faith." The law was never going to save anyone; the law was to make us mindful of sin. Paul wrote in **Galatians 3:24,** "The law, then, was our guardian until Christ, so that we could be justified by faith."

So you ask, "What was the way to salvation in the Old Testament?" Paul writes in **Romans 4:3,** "For what does the scripture say? Abraham believed in God, and it was credited to him for righteousness." Abraham had faith. God is love, and to demonstrate how much your soul meant to Him, He bankrupted heaven for you and me by sending His only son to save us from sin.

Jesus: Son of God

When you think of Jesus, what is your first thought? Fictional or Real? Many people have a relationship with Jesus, and others disregard who he is. I often wonder what could cause someone to turn away from a man who never sinned, died for the people of this world, and is the Son of God. Don't get me wrong, I was once that person. My truth: I didn't take the time to find out who Jesus was and is.

The Bible has been around for approximately 3,500 years. It is also referred to in scripture as the book of Law in **Deuteronomy 31:26,** the gospel in **Romans 1:16,** the Holy Scriptures in **Romans 1:2,** the instruction of the Lord in **Psalm 19:7,** the living oracles in **Acts 7:38,** the word of Christ, in **Colossians 3:16,** the Scroll in **Psalm 40:7,** the sword of the Spirit in **Ephesians 6:17**, and the word of life in **Philippians 2:16.** Whatever you chose, Jesus is your salvation.

Jesus of Nazareth, our living hope, to whom he has many names—Messiah, Emmanual, Yahweh, King, Friend, Lamb of God, was born over two thousand years ago. The son of Jewish parents named Mary and Joseph. We learn in **Matthew 1:21,** "She (Mary) will give birth to a son, and you are to name him Jesus, because he will save his people from their sins." For many, I'm sure it is unfathomable to grasp how any of that would be possible, but with God, all things are possible.

As a child and young adult, Jesus studied under his earthly father, Joseph, as a trade carpenter before the people knew him as the Messiah. It wasn't until he was thirty that his ministry took place over three years, and during that time, he sought twelve men who would become his disciples to help him spread his message of salvation. Jesus' first public miracle occurred in Cana during a wedding in **John 2:1-11** when He turned water into wine.

Jesus came to earth to please God the Father. **Hebrews 10:5-7,** "Therefore, as he was coming into the world, he said: You did not desire sacrifice and offering, but you prepared a body for me. *You did not delight in whole burnt offerings and sin offerings. Then I said, "See- it is written about me in the scroll- I have come to do your will, God."*

Jesus preached and taught repentance to those who would listen. His longest and most widespread sermon was "The **Sermon on the Mount** in **Matthew 5:3-12.** Which included The Lord's Prayer and the Beatitudes. Standing among those who came to hear Him preach in Galilee, saying,

"Blessed are those who are poor in spirit, for the kingdom of heaven is theirs."

"Blessed are those who mourn, for they will be comforted."

"Blessed are the humble, for they will inherit the earth."

"Blessed are those who hunger and thirst for righteousness, for they will be filled."

"Blessed are the merciful, for they will be shown mercy."

"Blessed are the pure in heart, for they will see God."

"Blessed are the peacemakers, for they will be called sons of God."

"Blessed are those who are persecuted because of righteousness, for the kingdom of heaven is theirs."

"You are blessed when they insult you and persecute you and falsely say every kind of evil against you because of me. Be glad and rejoice, because your reward is great in heaven. For that is how they persecuted the prophets who were before you."

Jesus performed many miracles, such as healing Leapers, restoring sight to the blind, curing the paralytic, stopping a woman from bleeding after twelve years, casting out demons, and raising three people from the dead: the daughter of Jarius, the son of the widow in Nain, and Lazarus all while proclaiming His father in heaven for the people's salvation.

One of my favorite accounts in the Bible is about Jesus' love and friendship with Mary Magdalene, also known as Mary of Magdala. Here was a woman whom Jesus cast out seven demons, freeing her from captivity, where her life changed completely. Mary became a faithful friend of Jesus.

It is written that she helped support His ministry, bore witness to His crucifixion, was present for His burial, laid eyes on an empty tomb where the Son of God no longer lays, and was one of the first witnesses of His resurrection. Wow!

As much as Jesus did for the people, some still saw no reason to follow him or heed His message about forgiveness and salvation. Many of the religious leaders found His teaching insulting. Even some of His disciples turned their backs on Him. Apostle Peter denied Him three times, and

Judas had Him captured, sealing His fate on the cross by the hands of Romans.

I often grappled with why Jesus would choose Judas as a disciple, knowing he would betray Him, and then it occurred to me- the answer is in **John 13:18-19,** "I'm not speaking about all of you; I know those I have chosen. But the Scripture must be fulfilled: *The one who eats my bread has raised his heel against me.* I am telling you now before it happens, so that when it does happen you will believe that I am He."

On the final day of Jesus' death, Pilate (Roman governor of Judaea) handed Him over to be crucified. The cruelty that took place upon Jesus was horrific—being nailed to a cross in an area known as the Skull, which in Aramaic is called Golgotha. Pilate had a sign made that was put on the cross that read, "Jesus of Nazareth, The King Of The Jews." As the soldiers crucified Jesus, they took his clothes and divided them into four parts, a part for each soldier. Dressing Him in a scarlet robe, they twisted together a crown of thorns, placed it upon His head, and put a staff in His right hand to mock Him, saying, "Hail, King of the Jews." If that wasn't enough, they spat on him, took the staff, and kept hitting Him on the head.

John 19:30, "When Jesus had received the sour wine, he said, "It is finished." Then, bowing His head, He gave up his spirit. Even after Jesus' death, one of the soldiers pierced his side with a spear. Take a moment and let what you just read about the brutal death of a man who came to rescue you and me from sin resonate in your mind. Heartbreaking, right? He shed his blood to set us free. Imagine those who loved Jesus, their hearts broken and tears on their face. Joseph of Arimathea and Nicodemus took care of Jesus' body, laying it in a tomb. Here's where the story turns around: this wasn't the end. Three days later, He had risen. He's alive! Hallelujah! He's alive!

I encourage every person who claims to know Jesus Christ, the Son of God, to be the hands and feet of our Savior. But if you are still learning what it means to put Christ first, that is okay, too. Even the most devout followers of Christ have stumbled and questioned their faith. What matters is that you **Seek**, and you shall find a God who loves you first.

He is unconditional love. Trusting and following Jesus will be a forever adventure, but it is worth it because He's coming back soon. Let's be ready together.

3. Salvation

Acts 4:12

"There is salvation in no one else, for there is no other name under heaven given to people by which we must be saved."

<u>Salvation</u>

When we speak of salvation in the bible, what do we mean? To understand, let us take a step back. Many people worldwide say it is ludicrous to believe, repent, and be baptized, all to serve a God we cannot see or genuinely know exists. With that being said, I can understand your skepticism. But how many of you or other people you know have taken a manufactured penny you can see, tossed it into a fountain, and somehow thought it would grant you a wish? Ludicrous?

I can boldly say that Jesus, God's Son, did exist. He was a man who knew no sin. The shortest verse in the bible is what I believe to be the most profound scripture: **John 11:35,** "Jesus wept." It allows us to connect with Him more profoundly. A man who loved people had compassion, healed, and, most notably, came to proclaim God the Father for our salvation. Jesus knew what He would endure for us, yet He went willing. Would you?

The Bible is about God dwelling with us and how we receive our place in heaven. So, what does salvation mean for us? Salvation means being rescued by God's grace, forgiving us of our sins so that we may have eternal life. In the Lord's prayer, we must understand that "Your kingdom come. Your will be done on earth as it is in heaven" is about salvation. Jesus taught this prayer so you may know God does not dwell just in heaven; he also resides within you through the Holy Spirit.

You cannot be saved for what you've done or what you have. No amount of good works can ever make up for our sins. What saves you is having a relationship with Jesus Christ, the Son of God. In **John 14:6,** Jesus declares, "I am the way, the truth, and the life. No one comes to the Father except through me."

Salvation is what we all need. **Romans 10:9-10** declares, "If you confess with your mouth, "**Jesus is Lord**," and believe in your heart that God raised him from the dead, you will be saved. One believes with the heart, resulting in righteousness, and one confesses with the mouth, resulting in salvation." Pray for *forgiveness by repenting* and acknowledging that you are a sinner. When you enter into a relationship with God, it's the most remarkable exchange in the world.

We get to give Him everything we possess, and He gives us everything He has and is. Who wouldn't want to trade their sin for righteousness or suffering for peace? He is the friend who will never leave you. The chains that have bound you for so long will no longer be. Seek Jesus for salvation through your faith, and watch your life change with His mercy and grace. **In John 8:36,** Jesus tells us, "So if the Son sets you free, you really will be free."

4. Ask, Seek, Knock

Matthew 7:7

"Ask, and it will be given to you. Seek, and you will find. Knock, and the door will be opened to you."

Ask, Seek, Knock

Jesus Christ, who intercedes on our behalf for the Father, assures us that if we "**Ask**," it will be given. Many people reject Jesus, accusing Him of being a liar when they do not receive what they have requested in prayer. Persistent prayer is what Jesus spoke about. In **Ephesians 6:18,** "Pray at all times in the Spirit with every prayer and request, and stay alert with all perseverance and intercession for all the saints." God speaks these words so you may not harden your heart, but remember that He hears all prayers and answers them according to His will, not yours. He knows what you need.

There are many factors in scripture as to why prayers are not answered.

1. **Psalm 66:18:** "If I had been aware of malice in my heart, the Lord would not have listened."

2. **Isaiah 59: 1-2:** "Indeed, the Lord's arm is not too weak to save, and his ear is not too deaf to hear. But your iniquities are separating you from your God, and your sins have hidden his face from you so that he does not listen."

3. **Proverbs 29:9,** "Anyone who turns his ear away from hearing the law-even his prayer is detestable."

4. **1 Peter 3:12,** "Because the eyes of the Lord are on the righteous and his ears are open to their prayer. But the face of the Lord is against those who do what is evil."

How do we right our wrongs so God can hear our prayers effectively? **Confess**! If we confess our sins, He is faithful to forgive. When we admit our offenses to God and ask for His forgiveness, He hears our petition and restores us.

Jeremiah 29:11: "For I know the plans I have for you- this is the Lord's declaration- "plans for your well-being, not for disaster, to give you a future and a hope."

The Son of God declares in **Matthew 6:8**, "Don't be like them, because your Father knows the things you need before you ask him." He has your best interests at heart and will answer according to His will, not yours. Why? Because He knows what is good and pleasing for your life. Having faith in the Father allows you to accept the outcome.

Psalm 105:4 reads, "**Seek** the Lord and his strength; **seek** his face always." When we seek Jesus, our heart draws near Him, comforting us and allowing for a more personal relationship with Him. Salvation is critical to reaching God the Father in heaven, and Jesus' sole purpose has always been to **seek** and save the lost so that we may have that chance. Spending more time in God's word will allow you to see the map of Jesus's heart for His children.

If you are not promised tomorrow, why would you gamble the greatest gift God gave you? Your soul. In **Matthew 24:44**, Jesus writes, "This is why you are also to be ready, because the Son of Man is coming at an hour you do not expect." As the body of Christ, we must continuously **seek** God to prepare us.

If you are new to learning what it means to love and follow Christ, the Bible affirms that the God of peace will be with you every step when you receive Him into your life without reservation. Being available to God is an essential part of your daily life. **Proverbs 8:17,** "I love those who love me, and those who search for me find me." Many times, people want the reward without having to put in the work. God deserves all of you. Nothing should separate your love for Him.

For God to sacrifice His son on the cross to die for your sins should be enough for you to spend time in God's word daily. People of this world ask for much more than God asks of you. The choice is yours because He has given you the free will to choose Him or the world. My path is the Jesus way; what do you prefer?

Over the years, as I study more about Jesus, I have realized that He has always been there. Our Jesus is so gracious that He asks for a seat at our table, unlike the devil, who takes it upon himself to slither his way into the lives of those who are most vulnerable. We are to look for the narrow path to Jesus's heart, which leads to humility and grace.

Romans 12:2 states, "Do not conform to this age, but be transformed by the renewing of your mind, so that you may discern what is the good, pleasing, and perfect will of God."

If we seek things of this world rather than our Savior, Jesus Christ, we allow our salvation to be in peril. What is so important about our salvation? Everything. Let us dive right into scripture. **John 3:16** has been the cornerstone of all believers and unbelievers. If I took a census on the number one scripture people know, it is this one, **"For God loved the world in this way: He gave his one and only Son, so that everyone who believes in him will not perish but have eternal life."**

Salvation brings eternal life. This begins with faith. Many people have asked me how to put trust in something that cannot be seen. We do not see the air but know it is there. In **John 3:8,** Jesus declares, "The wind blows where it pleases, and you hear its sound, but you don't know where it comes from or where it is going. So it is with everyone born of the spirit." When the spirit lives inside you, it produces a believer's clear and precise life. The will of the Father transforms the heart. **Romans 8:28,** "We know that all things work together for the good of those who love God, who are called according to his purpose." When we strive to be more like Christ, we can do good works in the Father's name.

In Revelations 3:20, Jesus reminds us, "See! I stand at the door and **knock**. If anyone hears my voice and opens the door, I will come into him and eat with him, and he with me." When we hear Jesus knocking, do we always answer, or are we ashamed of our sins? Offering Jesus a seat at our table and praising Him in the highest should never impede us. If we have faith the size of a mustard seed, we should know our God can do remarkable things. Praying daily for forgiveness will never cause hesitation to open the door to Jesus.

Nothing is too big for Jesus to handle, but you must give Him all you have. We cannot proclaim that He can make a way for us, yet give Him only what we choose. Doubting Jesus' ability hinders the very thing He died for. You! He is the truth, the way, the life. **John 20:29**, Jesus reveals, "Because you have seen me, you have believed. Blessed are those who have not seen and yet believe."

Wow! That is strong faith. If we stop and see the big picture of who Christ is and what He wants for us, it will be apparent that He is Love.

5. Grace

Ephesians 2:8-9

"For you are saved by grace through faith, and this is not from yourself; it is God's gift- not from works, so that no one can boast."

Grace

Grace is God's favor and kindness toward you. It is what the foundation of the bible is built on. **2 Timothy 1:9 says**, "He has saved us and called us with a holy calling, not according to our works, but according to his own purpose and grace, which was given to us in Christ Jesus before time began." What a powerful declaration. Even before we existed, God knew our needs—a savior to rescue us from sin. God knew this world needed Jesus Christ's life, death, and resurrection to redeem humanity.

The best grace is when God descended His son to earth, shedding His blood on the cross for sins to be forgiven. This immense gift is given to those who believe in Christ, yet we do not deserve it. We have all sinned and continue to sin.

Even when we have good intentions of not sinning, we find ourselves sinning, but this is where repentance comes in.

All past, present, and future sins are forgiven when you believe and trust in Christ enough to ask for forgiveness. Living in a wicked world will lead you down the wrong path, but learning righteousness takes real commitment. Studying God's word and allowing the Holy Spirit to guide you daily will help you grow your relationship with Jesus.

In this world, sin comes effortlessly, but doing what pleases God somehow is a challenge. Applying God's word throughout your life will remind you that He is a prayer away, and when you do not have the words, the Holy Spirit will intercede on your behalf. Learning forgiveness will help your mind and soul live better daily. Forgiving what someone has done to you might not change that person, but it changes you.

Allowing yourself to seek revenge is not what God wants for you. **Proverbs 24:29** reads, Don't say," I'll do to him what he did to me; I'll repay the man for what he has done." Forgiving grace indeed needs to be accompanied by God's strength. We alone will not overcome. The beauty of God's grace is that each day is anew. Yesterday's mistakes are no longer when you ask for forgiveness. This allows your heart and attitude to be refreshed. Observing God's beauty when you awake, smiling at your co-worker, lending help to a friend in need, and praying for someone is all about living your best life, and that's what God wants for you.

God's grace also frees your soul from others who might make you feel less of yourself. God is the only one you can take refuge in when this world's sins try to consume you or someone criticizes you. **Psalm 139:14**, "I will praise you because I have been remarkably and wondrously made. Your works are wonderous, and I know this very well." As you learn more about God in the Bible, you will know He makes no mistakes. **Proverbs 30:5** says, "Every word of God is pure; he is a shield to those who take refuge in him."

Your future is not of this world; it is with God and His infinite grace that will carry you. You will never be alone in your trials. **Romans 5:3- 5** declares, "And not only that, but we also boast in our afflictions, because we know that affliction produces endurance, endurance produces proven character, and proven character produces hope. This hope will not disappoint us, because God's love has been poured out in our hearts through the Holy Spirit given to us." Jesus informs us that we will suffer in this sinful world, but be courageous, for He has conquered the world.

You will find in scripture that **Genesis 6:8** declares, "Noah, however, found favor (grace) with the LORD." The word grace has been written in the bible over a hundred fifty times, **Revelations 22:21** being the last scripture; Apostle John ended the Bible with: "The grace of the Lord Jesus be with everyone. Amen."

6. Faith

Hebrews 11:1

"Now faith is the reality of what is hoped for, the proof of what is not seen."

Faith

Jesus Christ promises hope and salvation given by grace through faith in Him. It is easy to lose faith when experiencing overwhelming situations and feeling like God has left you to deal with it alone. You find yourself asking, "Where are you, God? I have been faithful. Why have you left me in my time of need?" **Isaiah 41:10,** God promises his people, "Do not fear, for I am with you; do not be afraid, for I am your God. I will strengthen you; I will help you; I will hold on to you with my righteous right hand."

Jesus never said that life would be stress-free when you take up your cross and follow Him. In **John 16:33,** Jesus says, "I have told you these things so that in me you may have peace. *You will have suffering* in this world. Be courageous! I have conquered the world." Your life will still have many challenges, but the good news is that you have victory in Jesus Christ. I want to share this insightful way of thinking when we wonder how we will get through the storms.

A Christian singer named Micah Tyler, who has several hit albums, quoted this at the beginning of his music video called **Different**; while among his trials, the prayer he kept asking was, "Jesus, can you just change these things? Can you stop the storms?" But He chose not to stop them just yet. Micah realized that the best question was not, "Jesus, can you change these things around me, but instead, God, can you change me so I can handle the things you are walking me through?"

Proverbs 24:10 reminds us, "If you do nothing in a difficult time, your strength is limited." When challenging times arise, and yes, they will, remember to continue loving Jesus and walking with Him. Keep His commandments. Prayer is vital in all circumstances. There is nothing God cannot handle. God wants all of you, and He does not deserve you to be a part-time follower of Him.

Many of you know what I mean. We should not consider Jesus our Lord and Savior only when it appeases us. He did not die on the cross, so His life would be in vain. Calling upon the Lord only when it suits you does not make you Christ-like; it makes you a hypocrite. Jesus bore your sin and shame, so you should gladly wear His name. Do as it is written in **2 Timothy 4: 2-5**, "Preach the word; be ready in season and out of season; correct, rebuke, and encourage with great patience and teaching. For the time will come when people will not tolerate sound doctrine, but according to their own desires, will multiply teachers for themselves because they have an itch to hear what they want to hear. They will turn away from hearing the truth and will turn aside to myths. But as for you, exercise self-control in everything, endure hardship, do the work of an evangelist, fulfill your ministry."

In the Bible, Jesus references a mustard seed to faith. What was He trying to convey? Even if your faith is the size of a mustard seed and you placed it with God, remarkable things will happen. **Hebrews 11:6,** "Now without faith it is impossible to please God, since the one who draws near to him must believe that he exists and that he rewards those who **seek** him."

When you petition God in your prayers, remember not to doubt, for it is written in **James 1:5-7,** "Now if any of you lacks wisdom, he should ask God- who gives to all generously and ungrudgingly- and it will be given to him. But let him ask in faith without doubting. For the doubter is like the surging sea, driven and tossed by the wind. That person should not expect to receive anything from the Lord, being double-minded and unstable in all his ways."

Genuine faith is not about how much work you have done but how honest and sincere you are through it. It will show how you obey in Jesus Christ. Step out in your faith. Be strong and courageous, for God is with you.

7. Church

Hebrews 10:24-25

"And let us consider one another in order to provoke love and good works, not neglecting to gather together, as some are in the habit of doing, but encouraging each other, and all the more as you see the day approaching."

Church

The Greek word ekklesia has been translated from original scriptures as the word church in the New Testament. The meaning of this word is assembly or congregation. It is written in many scriptures that we are to gather to learn God's word and fellowship. **Matthew 18:20**, Jesus declares, "For where two or three are gathered together in my name, I am there among them." If you follow Christ or are curious about your salvation in Christ, I will tell you that attending a church and fellowshipping with others is what God wants for you.

Although we may not know when Jesus will return, we must encourage one another in our walk of faith. Remember, the church is not the only place we can gather. Inviting others into your home for prayer and the Lord's supper is a beautiful way to fellowship. Small acts of kindness go a long way toward others.

The Lord's Supper

Luke 22:19-20

And he took bread, gave thanks, broke it, gave it to them, and said, "This is my body, which is given for you. Do this in remembrance of me." In the same way, he also took the cup after supper and said, "This cup is the new covenant in my blood, which is poured out for you."

Congregating together as a Body of Christ can do wonders for your soul. Hearing God's word preached can change your attitude, lifestyle, heart, and mind. Everyone sitting in a pew is a sinner, and no one is righteous. **Romans 3:23** reminds us, "For all have sinned and fall short of the glory of God." There have been many studies on why people may not attend church.

    1. They regard the church to be irrelevant.

    2. They cite the hypocrisy and moral failures of church leaders.

3. They feel God is missing in the church.

4. They do not feel spiritually fed.

I was once that person. I spent many years in and out of the church, asking myself why I attended church if it did not bring me peace and spiritual knowledge. I was taught that we need each other to build friendships and have people who will encourage us, teach us, and hold us accountable. When you find the right church, you will feel optimistic; you will have a greater understanding of your purpose in life, better self-control in your actions, and feel more connected to God.

It does matter what church you attend. If you walk into a church feeling broken, wanting to be spiritually fed, and you leave hungry for more of God's word that says something about that church, but if you go there several times and still feel broken, try another church. God will place you where you need to be. Find a church where people genuinely **seek** to know Christ and care for you. Church is for the broken looking to be healed through Jesus Christ. Affirmation that God cares for them.

We must remember that the church belongs not to the members but to Jesus. When we ask ourselves what kind of church Jesus wants, we can find it clearly in **Revelation 2:2-3.** "I know your works, your labor, and your endurance, and that you cannot tolerate evil people. You have tested those who call themselves apostles and are not, and you have found them to be liars. I know that you have persevered and endured hardships for my name's sake, and you have not grown weary."

Jesus wants a church that thirsts His word so that when you disciple others, they will also thirst His word, just as He proclaimed to the **Woman At The Well**, "Everyone who drinks from this water will get thirsty again. But whoever drinks from the water that I will give him will never thirst again. In fact, the water I will give them will become a well of water springing up in him for eternal life."

We can encourage others toward love and good deeds when we gather together. The Bible teaches us that the church is Christ's body. **Ephesians 1:22-23,** "And *he subjected everything under his feet* and appointed him as head over everything for the church, which is his body, the fullness of the one who fills all things in every way." Each person is a different body part that is intricately knitted together. **Ephesians 4:15-16,** "But speaking the truth in love, let us grow in every way into him who is the head- Christ. From him the whole body, fitted and knit together by every supporting ligament, promotes the growth of the body for building itself up in love by the proper working of each individual part."

Believers in Christ have the Holy Spirit, which draws them to God's church in unity. The Spirit yearns for us to gather in the House of the Lord. We are meant to share laughter and sorrow and be able to help one another. Singing together glorifies God, which always expresses our love for Him. Every day, we witness the struggles of co-workers, neighbors, strangers, and family. Those who are going through loss, addiction, health issues, marriages, and more will suffer in silence.

Being faithful Christians also means stepping outside the church and reaching out to those who cannot attend church. Just because we can sit at home and easily stream church on TV doesn't excuse us from not gathering with His saints in the church. If the pastor preaches God's word with conviction and love taken right out of the Bible, then he is being God's shepherd and preparing his flock for the coming of the Messiah.

Reaching out to those and offering hope can change a person's outlook for tomorrow. Inviting them to church and sharing God's word is what kindness and love looks like when you know Christ. If the church is filled with the Spirit, you will come as you are but won't stay as you are. Never walk away from where God intended you to gather and help change lives. Church.

8. Forgiveness

Ephesians 4:32

"And be kind and compassionate to one another, forgiving one another, just as God also forgave you in Christ."

Forgiveness

When Jesus carried that cross to Calvary, it was to set us free and forgive us of our sins, so who are we not to forgive others? The Son of God, a sinless man, proclaimed in **Matthew 5:44-45,** "But I tell you, love your enemies and pray for those who persecute you, so that you may be children of your Father in heaven." Forgiving someone may not necessarily change the person who did you wrong, but it will change you. It relieves you from not letting anger fester and consume you.

Jesus knew it would be challenging for us sometimes to turn the other cheek when someone has lied, betrayed, or even cursed us, so He declared, "For if you forgive others their offenses, your heavenly Father will forgive you as well. But if you don't forgive others, your Father will not forgive your offenses," **Matthew 6:14-15**. He wants your soul to be at peace. To live the life Jesus envisioned, you must learn to let go. When you pray to God, ask Him to help you work through the things that have kept you shackled so that He can break those chains. Doing so will allow you to move forward in your life. Forgiveness will be a constant part of your life, but it will be easier to work through with Christ.

Many who cannot utterly understand Jesus' sacrifice for their sins will have difficulty forgiving others, and Satan enjoys just that. Set your heart toward Jesus' forgiveness, and you will know how to forgive others in time. When Christ forgave, it was on the cross. The blood He shed covered your sins, and forgiveness was paid.

Crucified between Two Criminals

We read in **Luke 23:32-43** about two criminals being executed with Jesus. One was to the left, and the other to the right. One of the men insulted Christ, saying, "Aren't you the Messiah? Save yourself and us!" Yet the other man proclaimed his transgressions and believed he was being punished justly for his crimes. Accepting Jesus was the Messiah, he pleaded with these words, "Jesus, remember me when you come into your kingdom." Responding to the man,

Jesus declared, "Truly I tell you, today you will be with me in paradise." That is forgiveness.

Surrendering to God allows us to hand our hurt over to Him. He is love. He is merciful. He is compassionate. He makes a way. When we cannot let go of the hurt done to us, we look for ways to hurt back. Still, scripture states in **1 Samuel 24:15,** "May the Lord judge between you and me, and may the Lord take vengeance on you for me, but my hand will never be against you." Letting God be the judge so our hearts are not hardened by bitterness is better.

Finding peace for ourselves means allowing God to work on our hearts. As God's people, we continuously pray for mercy, so we should remember to be merciful toward others. Forgiveness does not mean what someone did is okay. It signifies you are learning what having Christ in your heart means.

Reference:

Genesis 37 through 50

The life of Joseph demonstrates redemption and forgiveness as to what it's like to have God's grace when your faith never wavers. Joseph's brothers, being jealous of him, sold him into slavery. Knowing God's presence was always with him, Joseph found forgiveness for his brothers when he finally came face to face with them. Instead of harboring anger toward them, he declared to his brothers that this was God's plan so that he may save many lives. **Romans 8:18,** "For I consider that the sufferings of this present time are not worth comparing with the glory that is going to be revealed to us." This verse reminds us of Joseph's story.

9. Humility

1Peter 5:6

"Humble yourself, therefore, under the mighty hand of God, so that he may exalt you at the proper time."

Humility

Jesus Christ displayed humility toward the Father and now sits at the right hand of God in heaven. In the bible, Jesus speaks about humbling yourself over thirty times. One of my favorite scriptures is **Matthew 11:29,** "Take my yoke upon you and learn from me, because I am lowly and humble in heart, and you will find rest for your souls." Coming to Jesus in prayer is a beautiful way to keep you humble. It's a reminder that you can't carry the burden alone.

God dislikes pride but welcomes humility. When the Holy Spirit dwells within you, you will live differently. Your actions toward others will become more gracious and forgiving. You will be more humble, realizing your needs are no more important than someone else's, and giving from the heart without expecting anything in return will bring you joy. **James 4:6,** "But he gives greater grace. Therefore, he says:

God resists the proud but gives grace to the humble." You can have a healthier relationship with your family and spouse when you love yourself entirely and learn to live humbly.

In today's world, the human race is a beautiful train wreck that we seem to ignore. Turning on the television and reading the news feed on our devices shows us that sin is among us, yet we continue doing our business daily as if things will change. It is written in **Hebrews 13:8,** "Jesus Christ is the same yesterday, today, and forever." We are the ones who need to be effective in the world. God calls upon His people to be compassionate toward others, love fervently without ceasing, and pray for those in need.

If we understand how Jesus displayed humility toward others, we can also set our eyes on living this way. **Philippians 2:3-4**, "Do nothing out of selfish ambition or conceit, but in humility consider others as more important than yourself. Everyone should look not to his own interest, but rather to the interest of others." Imagine the King of Heaven taking form as a servant man and humbling himself by becoming obedient to God the Father. Jesus was a perfect example of humility. He never mistreated those who did him wrong, yet he continued interceding on their behalf, asking the Father to forgive them.

Remember, pride leads us to sin; humility leads us to Christ. Jesus will help you live humbly if you ask Him so that you can focus on pointing others toward Him. In your daily prayer, ask God to remove pride where it dwells in your life and replace it with humility. Jesus tells us a parable of two men: one who boasts and the other who is humble. **Luke 18:10-14,** "Two men went up to the temple to pray, one a Pharisee and the other a tax collector. The Pharisee was standing and praying like this about himself: 'God, I thank you that I'm not like other people-greedy, unrighteous, adulterers, or even like this tax collector. I fast twice a week; I give a tenth of everything I get.' "But the tax collector, standing far off, would not even raise his eyes to heaven but kept striking his chest and saying, 'God, have mercy on me, a sinner!' I tell you, this one went down to his house justified rather than the other, because everyone who exalts himself will be humbled, but the one who humbles himself will be exalted."

Remember, the Lord looks upon those with favor who look toward Him with a humble heart and are sinners rather than those who have done charitable deeds with a puffed-up chest and a spirit of pride.

10. Baptism

Matthew 28:19

"Go, therefore, and make disciples of all nations, baptizing them in the name of the Father and of the Son and of the Holy Spirit."

Baptism

What is baptism? Those who follow Christ know that when you are baptized, you identify with Jesus' death, burial, and resurrection. It demonstrates obedience to Jesus and shows the world that you profess faith in Him. Baptism is not for salvation. Salvation is by grace through faith alone in Jesus Christ, not by works. **(Ephesians 2:8-9)** People who proclaim to have accepted Christ as their Savior get baptized because they have repented their sins and profess to trust and follow Christ.

Baptism does not mean we are perfect when we go under the water and come out of it. It symbolizes that your life will be anew. **Romans 6:4**. "Therefore we were buried with him by baptism into death, in order that, just as Christ was raised from the dead by the glory of the Father, so we too may walk in newness of life." You are no longer bound to your past sins. You have the power through Christ to defeat worldly desires that cripple you.

We know Christ was a sinless man who didn't need to be baptized, yet He asked John the Baptist to baptize Him. Ever wonder why? **Matthew 3:15,** Jesus answered him, "Allow it for now, because this is the way for us to fulfill all righteousness." When Jesus was baptized, He prayed, and while praying, heaven opened, and the Holy Spirit descended upon him in physical appearance like a dove. A voice from heaven called out, "You are my beloved Son; with you I am well-pleased."

Isaiah 11:2 states, "The Spirit of the LORD will rest on him- a Spirit of wisdom and understanding, a Spirit of counsel and strength, a Spirit of knowledge and the fear of the LORD." Jesus being baptized affirmed that the Holy Spirit and God declared He was the Messiah people had been waiting for.

2Corithians 5:17, "Therefore, if anyone is in Christ, he is a new creation; the old has passed away, and see, the new has come!" The life you were living of sin and shame is no longer. You have a new life, a new way of thinking, and acting as a follower of Christ. You are receiving His grace, His forgiveness, and His love. Baptism is an external sign of an internal decision to receive God's love and the Holy Spirit that will dwell within you. Some will debate that being baptized is unnecessary to be a believer in Christ. Still, I say to you: if you truly walk with Christ and go by scripture and not cherry-pick what pleases you, you will be obedient to Jesus' words when He says, "Be baptized in the name of the Father, the Holy Spirit, and the Son."

11. Sin

1John 1:8-10

"If we say, "We have no sin," we are deceiving ourselves, and the truth is not in us. If we confess our sins, he is faithful and righteous to forgive us our sins and to cleanse us from all unrighteousness. If we say, "We have not sinned," we make him a liar, and his word is not in us."

<u>Sin</u>

What does sin mean to you? The definition of sin is an immoral act. We can never escape sin but try to be less sinful each day. **Psalm 51:5,** "Indeed, I was guilty when I was born; I was sinful when my mother conceived me." Non-believers disagree with being born already having sinned, and people who believe in Christ believe you are born of sin. Scripture teaches us that Adam and Eve were the first people to cause sin in the world, but they were not the first to rebel against God. Satan, who some refer to as the devil, did just that.

Many people have described the devil as once an angel, but nowhere in the bible does it describe Satan as the word (angel), but it does tell him as a guardian cherub. The definition of cherub states, "a winged angelic being." Either way, he rebelled against God, causing him to be cast out of heaven, and yet God, being omniscient, must have known this would occur, so why did He let it? This had to be part of His sovereign plan, making way for our Savior.

1 John 3:8, "The one who commits sin is of the devil, for the devil has sinned from the beginning. The Son of God was revealed for this purpose: to destroy the devil's works." Life might have been played out differently if the devil had never existed, but then we would question God's plan for us and claim we know better than Him. In turn, we would be claiming we are above God.

People will claim that God set Adam and Eve up when He told them not to eat from the Tree of Knowledge of Good and Evil. **James 1:13,** No one undergoing a trial should say, "I am being tempted by God," since God is not tempted by evil, and he himself doesn't tempt anyone." The truth is that Adam and Eve had free will and chose disobedience that led to sin.

God's purpose and plan for humankind were set into motion. The simple truth is that sin is an affliction. Sin is destructive in many ways. It destroys family relationships, marriages, and friendships. If you let it, it will ruin everything in your life. Sin should never be taken lightly. Sin takes control and is relentless when you allow it in all life situations. **Galatians 5:16-17,** "I say, then, walk by the Spirit, and you will certainly not carry out the desire of the flesh. For the flesh desires what is against the Spirit, and the Spirit desires what is against the flesh; these are opposed to each other, so that you don't do what you want."

Romans 8:38-39, "For I am persuaded that neither death nor life, nor angels nor rulers, nor things present nor things to come, nor powers, nor height nor depth, nor any other created thing will be able to separate us from the love of God that is in Christ Jesus our Lord." Let it be known that sin is the only thing that separates you from God, as written in **Isaiah 59:2,** "But your iniquities are separating you from your God, and your sins have hidden his face from you so that he does not listen."

Ever wonder how to decipher sin? God's word is evident in defining what's sinful with the text being in the bible. The Holy Spirit will steer you away from what is not pleasing to God. This is why it's crucial to have a relationship with God.

The one who sent His son for your sins. The one for whom we wait for—the one who loves us. **Romans 6:23,** "For the wages of sin is death, but the gift of God is eternal life in Christ Jesus our Lord." Repent of your sins. Trust and follow Christ. Let Him restore your soul.

1 Peter 5:8, "Be sober-minded, be alert. Your adversary the devil is prowling around like a roaring lion, looking for anyone he can devour." He (the devil) is attempting to lure souls into sin, causing chaos and havoc in your life. We must remember that things in this world will not last forever, but the love of Christ will.

Romans 16:20, "The God of peace will soon crush Satan under your feet. The grace of our Lord Jesus be with you." With Christ, we can put our heel on the devil's head, avoiding temptation, but we also have those who oppose God in the world to watch out. The world is threatening to Christians' followers. We are to expect people to tempt us to sin who don't understand or follow Christ.

Our flesh is weak, and desires sin over the spirit, so we must be cautious. We must remind ourselves to ask God to bring us out of evil. **Romans 8:13,** "Because if you live according to the flesh, you are going to die. But if by the Spirit you put to death the deeds of the body, you will live."

Sin is the work of the devil, and he will do anything to cover up God's love and truth so you suffer instead of prospering. Sin is what every person experiences daily and is not just the inner parts of us but also the outer parts.

Example:

Inner parts- Thoughts

Outer parts- Actions

We must know our intentions and motives in what we say and do. Sin will lead you to hell, and Jesus will lead you to heaven. The Spirit can help us overcome our weaknesses and live pleasing to God.

The Ten Commandments

1 You shall have no other gods before me.

2. You shall make no idols.

3. You shall not take the name of the Lord your God in vain.

4. Keep the Sabbath day holy.

5. Honor your father and mother.

6. You shall not murder.

7. You shall not commit adultery.

8. You shall not steal.

9. You shall not bear false witness against your neighbor.

10. You shall not covet.

Here is a fun fact about where people are in their lives with The Ten Commandments. If we were to randomly pick people and ask them to recite The Ten Commandments, they couldn't. Is it because many people think they do not apply anymore? Do we only go by the New Testament? Or is it because they don't know The Ten Commandments? I say it's because we, as a society, don't put God first in everything.

When I was around ten, I attended a church back up North for a few years with my parents called the International Church of the Nazarene. It was truly diverse. African Americans, Portuguese, Spanish, Creole, and Caucasians all attended. Everyone who walked through those doors had one purpose—making much of Jesus Christ. Fellowshipping was always enjoyable. God was in the room when everyone sang, clapping His hands to our voices. When service was over, and the preacher Rev. Manuel

Chavier extended his hand holding mine, I always remembered him saying, "I'm glad you're here. Remember, God loves you."

We can attend church anywhere, and God is with us, **Emmanuel**, but can we be with Him every day as we should? Back to the Ten Commandments, sorry, I digress. If we were to poll the same people, we randomly picked The Ten Commandments and asked them to name ten beers or ten of their favorite songs; I'm absolutely 100% sure they could over God's law. We **seek** a better life but don't **seek** the one who is able and willing to give it.

Am I guilty of the same thing? Yes. I wouldn't call out others unless I can boldly call myself out. And sure, most people say that God's law is common sense, yet we have at least broken one if not more. I have also had debates with people over said laws. My favorite conversation goes like this.

"Crystal, we know murder, stealing, sleeping with someone else's husband or wife is wrong. We don't need God to tell us that."

To say I have all the answers would be a lie, and I am not lying to anyone as I write this. What I will declare is that if you read early on in the Bible, when sin entered the world, it opened us all up to wrongful doings. Just as today, we have judge, jury, and execution.

In the Bible,
Adam and Eve disobeyed God the Father #5
Then we have Cain, who murdered his brother #6
King David, who committed adultery #7
King Solomon, who put other Gods before the Lord #1
Achan stole #8

My point is that in biblical times, and even now, these commandments are still being broken, yet I have been told they are common sense. We are all made in God's image and can use common sense, but that doesn't mean we do. The Ten Commandments are just as valid today as they were three thousand years ago when God gave them to Moses.

12. Love

1Corinthinans 13:4-7

"Love is patient, love is kind. Love does not envy, is not boastful, is not arrogant, is not rude, is not self-seeking, is not irritable, and does not keep record of wrongs. Love finds no joy in unrighteousness but rejoices in the truth. It bears all things, believes all things, hopes all things, endures all things."

Love

Love has many definitions, such as a feeling for someone or something, a pleasure in something, and a range of emotions, but beyond that, God is love. The Greatest Command Jesus spoke in the Bible is **Matthew 22:37,** *"Love the Lord your God with all your heart, with all your soul, and with all your mind."* The second is **Matthew 22:39**, *"Love your neighbor as yourself."* These scriptures are written so people may love God and their neighbor without reservation.

Some people today believe that God from the Old and New Testaments differ. Somehow, because of wars, judgment, and plagues back then, God is different today. But

James 1:17 declares, "Every good and perfect gift is from above, coming down from the Father of lights, who does not change like shifting shadows."

In the book Jonah, we learn that the Ninevites were one of the worst people, yet God had Jonah proclaim His word in hopes that they would repent. Jonah believed Nineveh would be demolished in forty days, but God saw they had turned away from their evil ways. In doing so, God relented from the disaster he had threatened them with. **Jonah 3:8-10.** God found mercy and love in humanity.

Isaiah 54:10, "Though the mountains move and the hills shake, my love will not be removed from you and my covenant of peace will not be shaken," says your compassionate Lord. The assurance of God's love. What a promise for all who trust in the Lord. God will protect and show love to those who believe in Him, but for those who do not, I pray for you. In the New Testament, God bankrupted heaven for us with His son, Jesus, who loved His people. Many accounts in the Bible show Jesus's love.

Jesus healed.

Matthew 4:24, "Then the news about him spread throughout Syria. So they brought to him all those who were afflicted, those suffering from various diseases and intense pains, the demon-possessed, the epileptics, and the paralytics. And he healed them. Today, we have the Holy Spirit healing physically, emotionally, and spiritually."

Jesus raised people from the dead.

Today, it's a different kind of raising he is doing. It's spiritual. He's giving new life to people who are putting their trust in him.

Jesus fed the hungry.

With only five barley loaves and two small fish, the people saw Jesus perform a miracle that would be enough to feed them and more. In **John 6:14,** the people proclaimed, "Surely, this is the Prophet who is to come into the world." He continues to feed us with the words in the bible to fill our hearts and souls.

Jesus intercedes for his flock.

John 17:20-21, Jesus prays, "I pray not only for these, but also for those who believe in me through their word. May they all be one, as you, Father, are in me and I am in you. May they also be in us so that the world may believe you sent me." Jesus knew his sheep (His people) would be dispersed after His crucifixion. He prayed for them continuously, knowing they were left in this sinful, fallen world. Many of them chose suffering and death in the name of Jesus.

Jesus gives His life for the world.

John 3:16 tells it all. Nothing can compare to the love that Jesus has. Nothing can stand up to what Jesus did 2,000 years ago for this world—living with sinful people, hoping they would not spend eternity separated from the Father in Heaven. We will never comprehend the magnitude of Jesus' love, but we can receive it and honor Him by obeying and loving Him.

13. Suffering

2Corinthians 1:3-4

"Blessed be the God and Father of our Lord Jesus Christ, the Father of mercies and the God of all comfort. He comforts us in all our affliction, so that we may be able to comfort those who are in any kind of affliction, through the comfort we ourselves receive from God."

Suffering

In this day and age, we see suffering the world continues to endure. We feel brokenhearted and discouraged that nothing will get better. Wars, starvation, homelessness, pandemics, child trafficking, economic turmoil, loss of a loved one. The list goes on. There is not one person who isn't affected by the realities of life. One of the most challenging questions in theology is, "Why do bad things have to happen?"

In the book of **Job 1:1,** in the country of Uz, there was a man named Job. He was a man of complete integrity who feared God and turned away from evil. Although he was a righteous man, God allowed Satan to do anything he wanted to Job except kill him. With that being said, Job didn't understand why God allowed these things, but he knew God was good and, therefore, continued to trust Him. You shake your head, saying, "This doesn't make sense."

This may be a hard pill to swallow, but there are no "good" people in the sense of the word itself. We all are corrupted by sin. **1 John 1:8,** If we say, "We have no sin," we are deceiving ourselves, and the truth is not in us." If you believe in Christ and yet bad things happen to you, take heart; this world is not the end. The inward parts of us are being renewed every day. What we suffer here is nothing compared to the glorious day we will have in heaven with the Father.

God uses your afflictions for good. You may not see nor understand at the moment, but everything that is difficult or seems not right in your life is a divine invitation to Him. Bad things will test your faith and your trust in Him. The scars you've endured and have overcome might help someone else get through their battles. No matter what grief you suffer on this earth, nothing can compare to Jesus's suffering on the cross for your sins.

God never promised we would not suffer, but if you remember that God is good, just, merciful, and loving, you will overcome the hurt. **Proverbs 3:5-6**, "Trust in the LORD with all your heart, and do not rely on your own understanding; in all your ways know him, and he will make your paths straight." God is interested in saving your soul. Apostle Paul called out to Jesus three times, asking for deliverance, but instead, in 2 **Corinthians 12:9,** Jesus replied, "My grace is sufficient for you, for my power is perfected in weakness."

God has a profound love for all people. Suffering is not always a punishment from God. **Romans 8:17,** "and if children, also heirs-heirs of God and coheirs with Christ-if indeed we suffer with him so that we may also be glorified with him." Part of being in Christ means you inherit what Christ has, not just glory but suffering. It molds us more into the image of Jesus spiritually.

Jeremiah 10:19, "Woe to me because of my brokenness- I am severely wounded! I exclaimed, "This is my intense suffering, but I must bear it." During the grief and suffering, God is there. The Bible says we should be content in our suffering. Paul suffered, and it strengthened him. We may not understand everything, but we should worship and pray to Jesus, saying, "I don't understand it all, but I believe you are great and merciful. I believe and trust in you. May my actions throughout my suffering still glorify you. Carry me through the storms so that I may help others who may also be suffering.

1 Peter 5:10, "The God of all grace, who called you to his eternal glory in Christ, will himself restore, establish, strengthen, and support you after you have suffered a little while." Suffering can teach you humility and grace and prepare you for glory. Apostle Paul writes in **2 Corinthians 4:17-18,** "For our momentary light affliction is producing for us an absolutely incomparable eternal weight of glory. So we do not focus on what is seen, but on what is unseen. For what is seen is temporary, but what is unseen is eternal."

Romans 8:31-32, "What, then, are we to say about these things? If God is for us, who is against us? He did not even spare his own Son but gave him up for us all. How will he not also with him grant us everything?" We can be confident that God is always assisting us in overcoming our difficulties.

14. Scripture

Romans 15:4

"For whatever was written in the past was written for our instruction, so that we may have hope through endurance and through the encouragement from the Scriptures."

Scripture

The Bible has sixty-six books and thirty-one thousand one hundred and three scriptures for us to navigate through life if we apply them to our lives. It is a map directly to Jesus's heart. Each author took the time to write what was seen and heard from God the Father and Jesus Christ, granting us a better future. The Bible is and will always be the best-selling book. One hundred million Bibles are printed yearly, and more than twenty million are sold.

If every person who read the bible applied the scriptures to their life, they would honestly know the presence of God. If you read but do not live out what God has instructed you to do, you have allowed yourself to walk mindlessly, feeling alone. There is so much to be seen in scripture. There is purpose in scripture, which points to authority, guidance, and inspiration, but it is also eternal. In **2 Timothy 3:16-17,** it is written, "All scripture is inspired by God and is profitable for teaching, for rebuking, for correcting, for training in righteousness, so that the man of God may be complete, equipped for every good work."

As you read scripture, it is good to memorize it as well so that the more you read and learn, the more you think and live the Jesus way. Scripture is spiritual food for your soul. You will grow and flourish in your walk with Christ. We should also teach our children so that they may grow in love with Christ and continue as they mature. **Joshua 1:8,** "This book of instruction must not depart from your mouth; you are to meditate on it day and night so that you may carefully observe everything written in it. For then you will prosper and succeed in whatever you do."

Some people give up reading scripture because it is too difficult to understand or overwhelming. Still, Jesus promises that the Holy Spirit will open your mind to understand the scriptures. If you hunger for the word of God, you will be fed.

15. Worship & Prayer

Psalm 95:6-7

"Come, let's worship and bow down; let's kneel before the Lord our maker. For he is our God, and we are the people of his pasture, the sheep under his care."

Worship & Prayer

When we worship the Lord, we are genuinely treasuring Him. We value Him in our life more than anything else. There are several ways we should worship God. When we serve, sing, tithe, and fellowship. Glorifying God is honestly what worshipping is. Prayer is the communication between you and the Father. It is a lifeline to the one who loved you first. He waits for you to call out, bearing your soul for Him to restore you, bringing you out of the storm.

Worship is loving God for His grace toward us. We should always worship God because this is the one thing we have to give Him, yet sometimes we put Him on the back burner because we don't want to take time for Him. Take a second and consider what would have happened if He hadn't died on the cross for your sins. Where would you be today?

Go out and spread God's message to others who may not know Him.

How do you win battles that are formed against you? Prayer. When you get down on your knees in prayer, you should always thank God for what He does in your life, even if you don't understand it. We are often burdened, yet we tell others we are good. We hold on to things that wear us down, but Jesus sees us exactly where we are. You can boldly bring all of your requests to the throne of God, trusting He can do remarkable things in your life.

God works miracles. I mean, jaw-dropping, can't comprehend it, miracles. In prayer, He is orchestrating the chapters in your story. With each passing day, we should pray fervently to God, thanking Him for His grace and love. What is so miraculous is that we can talk to Him anywhere. Your conversation with God never has to be elegant. Just be honest with what's in your heart. Thank Him for what He has already done and accomplished in your life.

We should also pray for the pastor, his family, the leadership team, and those who serve vigorously, helping the church grow in Christ. May we ask God to give the church a fresh outpouring of His Spirit. **2 Chronicles 7:14,** "And my people, who bear my name, humble themselves, pray and seek my face, and turn from their evil ways, then I will hear from heaven, forgive their sin, and heal their land." God makes it clear: Pray.

16. The Armor of God

Ephesians 6:10

"Finally, be strengthened by the Lord and by his vast strength."

The Armor of God

Apostle Paul writes in **Ephesians 6:11,** "Put on the full armor of God so that you can stand against the schemes of the devil." You have an enemy that is against you and is not for you. He will continuously try to provoke you so that you hide away instead of marveling at the victory that you have in Christ. However, we must remember that we need to stand firm. The devil is not made up; he's not fictitious. He will disguise himself so you forget he's lurking and waiting to cause chaos.

Your real enemy is unseen, and it's not a family member, a co-worker, or a friend. **Ephesians 6:12,** "For our struggle is not against flesh and blood, but against the rulers, against the authorities, against the cosmic powers of this darkness, against evil, spiritual forces in the heavens." The devil is making sure you're not walking pleasingly to the Lord. He has tactics, enticing you with anything when you're vulnerable. He does not want you to live for God.

Paul shares what we need to keep the devil at arm's length. **Ephesians 6:13-18,** "For this reason take up the full armor of God, so that you may be able to resist in the evil day, and having prepared everything, to take your stand. Stand, therefore, with truth like a belt around your waist, righteousness like armor on your chest, and your feet sandaled with readiness for the gospel of peace. In every situation take up your shield of faith with which you can extinguish all the flaming arrows of the evil one. Take the helmet of salvation and the sword of the Spirit- which is the word of God. Pray at all times in the Spirit with every prayer and request, and stay alert with all perseverance and intercession for all the saints."

All these are excellent weapons against the devil, but prayer is the most crucial weapon. How can we have victory if we don't pray every day? Prayer unlocks the source of heaven. Why would we wait until we get to heaven to experience all God has for us now? Praying is what keeps the devil away. **Luke 18:1,** "Now he told them a parable on the need for them to pray always and not give up."

The enemy will bend his knee at the power of prayer. You can pray every day, but if you do not live a life aligned with the truth of God, you've wasted your time praying. Don't let the Bible be ink on pages; let it be God's voice to you daily. The breastplate will keep the devil from getting to your heart. Wear the Armor of God so that you may prevail over the enemy.

17. Holy Spirit

Ephesians 1:13-14

"In him you also were sealed with the promised Holy Spirit when you heard the word of truth, the gospel of your salvation, and when you believed. The Holy Spirit is the down payment of our inheritance, until the redemption of the possession, to the praise of his glory."

Jesus knew his death was near, so in **John 14:15-17 he declared,** "If you love me, you will keep my commands. And I will ask the Father, and he will give you another counselor to be with you forever. He is the spirit of truth. The world is unable to receive him because it doesn't see him or know him. But you do know him, because he remains with you and will be in you." The Bible teaches us that the Holy Spirit, the Father, and the Son are the same—a trinity.

Psalm 139:7, "Where can I go to escape your Spirit? Where can I flee from your presence?" The Holy Spirit is everywhere. It will convict you of sin. But there is no situation you may be going through that the Holy Spirit can't realign you, bringing you back to Christ. When you receive

Jesus, you accept the Fruit of the Spirit, which gives you peace, joy, love, goodness, self-control, faith, and more. This happens through the Holy Spirit. These traits are of Jesus Christ. **Romans 8:6,** "Now the mindset of the flesh is death, but the mindset of the spirit is life and peace."

Without the Holy Spirit in you, you are eternally dead to God. Your body is living, but your spirit is not. Jesus stated that you must be born again. This will lead you from salvation to glorification. **2 Corinthians 13:13,** "The grace of the Lord Jesus Christ, and the love of God, and the fellowship of the Holy Spirit be with you all." The Holy Spirit is God's power in action in your life.

For God to fill you with the Holy Spirit, you must learn to forget about yourself and stop focusing on what you think excludes you from God's love and grace. Sometimes, we get in our way, which can obscure us from Jesus. **Galatians 5:25,** "If we live by the Spirit, let us also keep in step with the Spirit." You can only live godly and serve the Lord if you know how the Holy Spirit works. What does the Holy Spirit help us with? It helps us pray and worship, gives us boldness, performs miracles, teaches us the word, gives us faith, and continuously points us to Jesus.

The Holy Spirit assures you in your relationship that you are God's child adopted into the kingdom. You should be aware of walking with the Spirit of God every day. The Christian life means being submissive to the Holy Spirit for Jesus Christ living in and through you. This will ensure that you live a life of obedience.

You experience the world, flesh, and the devil at your doorstep daily. If you allow the Holy Spirit to guide you, He will always lead you to the right path; it will be up to you to take that path. The devil will always be there to mislead you and have you rebel against God. Set your mind on what the Spirit is guiding you toward. **Colossians 3:1-2,** "So if you have been raised with Christ, seek the things above, where Christ is, seated at the right hand of God. Set your minds on things above, not on earthly things."

When you don't read and meditate on the Word of God, you start to do things that are not of God. You become programmed to feed yourself with ungodly stuff. Starve the sin to death so that you can focus on God. The Holy Spirit will set your mind and enable you to do it. It is His will that you do it, and that's why the word of God is precious.

18. Hands & Feet

Matthew 5:16

"In the same way, let your light shine before others, so that they may see your good works and give glory to your Father in heaven."

Hands & Feet

As people, we become so focused on what we desire, what we don't possess, what we believe we need, or what people don't do for us that it blocks the joy, peace, and blessings that God has for us. Instead, we need to say, "God, while I'm waiting on my situation that I've prayed about, show me someone I may be a blessing to." The Bible says God knows what you need, so while you're waiting, bless someone else. **Galatians 5:13,** "For you were called to be free, brothers and sisters; only don't use this freedom as an opportunity for the flesh, but serve one another through love."

Colossians 3:23-24, "Whatever you do, do it from the heart, as something done for the Lord and not for people, knowing that you will receive the reward of an inheritance from the Lord. You serve the Lord Christ." However, many people miss the rewards from God because they only look for what people can do for them. Believe me, if you pray to God to show you what you can do for someone else, He will show you. If you are truly filled with the Spirit of God, you'll want to do for others.

Mark 10:23-25, "Jesus looked around and said to his disciples, "How hard is it for those who have wealth to enter the kingdom of God!" The disciples were astonished at his words. Again, Jesus said to them, "Children, how hard is it to enter the kingdom of God! It is easier for a camel to go through the eye of a needle than for a rich person to enter the kingdom of God." The lesson that Jesus wanted the disciples and all of us to learn is that whatever you give up for His sake, you will receive far more. You cannot outgive God.

We need to know what it's like to give. Generosity doesn't come naturally to all people, but selfishness does. When did you last do something for someone without them asking or wanting anything in return? Whenever we give, whether it's our time to someone, an offering at church, buying someone's groceries, or allowing someone to have our parking space, we become more like God in those moments. Think about it; that's what He does. He GAVE his only son.

It is beautiful to sponsor a child in another country, donate funds to our veterans, feed others, pay someone's bill, and give them a ride to the doctor. I pray we don't miss the opportunity to share the gospel with that individual. If we meet a person's physical needs but miss the chance at their spiritual needs, then we've missed all of what God has called us to do. Let's not only be His hands and feet but also his voice.

19. Death & Eternal Life

John 10:28-30

"I give them eternal life, and they will never perish. No one will snatch them out of my hand. My Father, who has given them to me, is greater than all. No one is able to snatch them out of the Father's hand. I and the Father are one."

Death & Eternal Life

Death is not the most enjoyable conversation to have or even think about when you have uncertainties about where you may spend eternity. Death will happen for all of us, and it's unavoidable. We should want to talk about this so that we end up in the right place when we die. Death on earth is just death. Your soul and spirit will go somewhere else, and there are two choices that you have: heaven or hell. I can't speak for you, but I chose heaven. The description of what Hell will be like is not a place anyone should want to spend eternity.

God's word describes hell of darkness, gnashing of teeth, fire, and separation from Him. **Jude 1:13,** "They are wild waves of the sea, foaming up their shameful deeds; wandering stars for whom the blackness of darkness is reserved forever." And in **Matthew 8:12,** "But the sons of the kingdom will be thrown into the outer darkness where there will be weeping and gnashing of teeth."

Those who don't know God are not aware of what will happen to them after they die. The Bible teaches us that once you die, you die. **Hebrews 9:27,** "And just as it is appointed for people to die once- and after this judgment." We will all answer to God. **Romans 14:12** clearly states, "So then, each of us will give an account of himself to God." One of the benefits of knowing Christ and following Him is that you don't have to fear death. This place is where we dwell until we are with the Father in heaven. It's temporary. So how do we know there's life after death? Jesus lived, died, and then rose again.

Eternal life is a gift. **Romans 6:23,** "For the wages of sin is death, but the gift of God is eternal life in Christ Jesus our Lord." The moment you believe in Jesus Christ as your Lord and Savior, your eternal life begins as told in **John 3:36,** "The one who believes in the Son has eternal life, but the one who rejects the Son will not see life; instead, the wrath of God remains on him. The word "has" is present. The question is whether you have eternal life or are you seeking to have eternal life.

If you **seek** eternal life, you must change your perception of who Jesus is. Faith will let you know who He is and what He did for you and the rest of the world when He hung on the cross. His death paid for our sins. **Acts 3:19- 20 says,** "Therefore repent and turn back, so that your sins may be wiped out, that seasons of refreshing may come from the presence of the Lord, and that he may send Jesus, who has been appointed for you as the Messiah."

When Christ hung on that cross, his nailed, scarred hands were payment for your past, and he wanted nothing more than for you to know his love. That day, the redemption of the world fell on his heart.

Jesus Christ is the only one who can save you from sin.

Acknowledgments

For those who Seek Him.

I pray that you (the reader) have found these words I have written to be uplifting and encouraging. If the Holy Spirit is tugging on your heart, and you feel the love of God, my heart is smiling for you. Giving your life to Christ will change how you feel, think, and act, bringing you peace. Never feel that you are too guilty, too far gone for His grace, and that it's too late. Jesus' blood says you are loved. You are made for more. Your debt has been paid.

Will you still stumble every day? Will you get knocked down?

Probably. But the difference is, you won't stay there because you have a Savior!

If you are ready to accept Jesus into your life, here is a prayer you can say silently to Jesus, "Heavenly Father, I come to you today to declare I am a sinner who needs a savior. I cannot do this on my own. I need your love and forgiveness. I want to live a life that is pleasing to you. Please transform my heart and life into your image so that my name is written in the Book of Life. I praise you for your love. Amen.

I want to share a sermon from my Pastor, Josh Taylor, at Mt. Carmel Baptist Church in Demorest, Georgia. I genuinely believe God places certain people in our lives so that they can teach us how to love like Jesus, so thank you to my church family for opening the doors to my family and saying, "Come as you are. You are loved."

Pastor Josh Taylor.

God loves you. He is the heartbeat of your life. A father who gave his only begotten son. A love so fierce, unfathomable, that he bore the weight of all your sins. **Romans 5:8,** "But God proves his love for us in that while we were still sinners, Christ died for us." The anguish of all of your pain and despair of all your sorrows, God says, "I'll take that." When you endure the pain and suffering and your sinful nature, your foolish, spiritually weak heart wants to question the love of God; you do this. You challenge every doubt and circumstance with the cross.

The cross is your assurance. The God who would give you Christ crucified will surely not deny you anything you need. The cross restores our faith in God's conquering presence and continuous provisions during suffering. It shows us that God is on our side. He takes a stand with us. Even when the circumstances appear adversarial, you can confidently say God is for me. You are held closer to the heart of God more than you can ever imagine. You are loved and cherished beyond understanding. Carry the cross in your heart. God gave you His absolute best. His one and only son to rescue you from despair and the clutches of sin.

This Is for You, Friend…

Luke 1:45 *"Blessed is she who has believed that the Lord would fulfill what he has spoken to her!"*

Many verses in the Bible genuinely describe the person you are, but this one stood out. Your faith and love for the Lord is beautiful. Growing personally and spiritually with you has enriched my life. Friendships are just one of the many gifts we have been given. Ours will last forever because we desire the same thing, **JESUS.** Empathy, love, and compassion with a lifetime of Jesus will flourish, and our friendships will be unbreakable. Friends who love Christ will weather the storm together, and each will keep the other on the path for Jesus. Thank you for being that friend.

With love… your sister in Christ.

Author Bio

Crystal Cattabriga lives in Georgia with her husband. Her passion for reading led her to write her first book in 2010, winning a Reader's Choice Award. Besides being an author, she has a degree in carpentry and nursing. When not plotting her next book, she spends her time reading, kayaking on the lake, fishing, and spending time with her family.

Recommendations for Christian Books, Music, and Movies

The Holy Bible
Phil Wickham - On our Knees
More Than a Carpenter – Josh & Sean McDowell
A Preach Well Church – Pastor Josh Taylor
Following Christ – Charles H. Spurgeon
The Power of Prayer – Charles H. Spurgeon

Christian Music Artist

Phil Wickham

Crowder

Toby Mac

Zach Williams

Austin French

Micah Tyler

Matthew West

Jeremy Camp

Family Faith Movies

BREAKTHROUGH

I CAN ONLY IMAGINE

THE HEALER

I STILL BELIEVE

WAR ROOM

LETTER TO GOD

THE SHACK

RUN THE RACE

PAUL - APOSTLE OF CHRIST

SON OF GOD